Healing:
Prayer
or Pills?

Jonathan G. Yoder, MD

HERALD PRESS
Scottdale, Pennsylvania
Kitchener, Ontario

HEALING: PRAYER OR PILLS?
Copyright © 1975 by Herald Press, Scottdale, Pa. 15683.
    Published simultaneously in Canada by Herald Press,
    Kitchener, Ont. N2G 1A7.
International Standard Book Number: 0-8361-1763-8
Library of Congress Catalog Card Number: 74-30988
Printed in the United States of America
Design by Alice B. Shetler

To the memory of
Dr. Mary Jean Yoder
who taught me so
much about faith

CONTENTS

PREFACE

I have often seen Christian people become frustrated and confused in times of serious illness because their understanding and faith regarding illness was not complete.

I have also had patients who thought they were at peace with God and man and had fully accepted their serious illness in faith. But some of the latter suddenly became alarmed and afraid. Well-intentioned friends planted seeds of doubt and distrust in the minds of the dying with the question, "How can you be sick *if* you are a Christian?"

I particularly remember a young woman with whom I had a lengthy conversation, knowing that she would be dead in a few days. "Friends" had harassed her, saying she must have unforgiven sin in her life or she wouldn't be sick. Her victory was in jeopardy. I told her repeatedly that we don't know all the meanings of sickness. We do know that God's children are subject to sickness and that God's grace is sufficient.

In my last conversation at her bedside she took my hand and said, "Please talk nice like that to me again." She needed reassurance of the love and mercy of God, in spite of adversity and sickness. Facing death, she wanted to be sure that her illness was not proof of an unforgiven soul. It was my privilege to help her regain the sustaining faith she needed for the hour of death.

I have seen repeated instances of this kind of misguided advice. Overly zealous Christians, who claim to have a special revelation, disturb genuine children of God in their hour of final crisis, when their needs for assurance are greatest.

I have also seen numerous tragic misunderstandings of the true nature of faith. A child has leukemia. The whole family has "faith" that the child will be cured. A man of God is called to see the child. After prayer and a healing service the child is pronounced "healed." Hopes are built higher and higher as the child becomes weaker and weaker and weaker. "Faith" holds fast, no matter what the appearance of the child! The parents affirm their faith more emphatically and more frantically. Then the child dies. What a terrible letdown! Where does one go next?

An ardent Christian missionary doctor told me how he and his wife went through this same cycle in China when their child became acutely ill and died. But his "faith" did not even stop at death. For hours he felt sure that Jesus would come in and say, "Little girl,

7

arise." But in the end Jesus did not come and raise her. They buried her in China. As he spoke, I sensed the intense suffering through which he had passed in this episode of his life almost fifty years before. Both he and I were aware of his present deeper and more mature faith and assurance. But I could not forget the deep hurt and despair which had struck him when his own little girl died. God had refused to heal her in spite of his prayers and a faith he thought could do anything. The scars were still with him.

Not long ago the parents of a small child in the United States were indicted for manslaughter. In "faith" they discontinued giving insulin to their diabetic child. The child had been pronounced "healed" by a Christian who had prayed over him, so they thought it would be the sin of unbelief to continue giving insulin. But in a few days the child was dead, and the parents faced a charge of manslaughter.

Such tragedies result from an incomplete understanding of the real cause of sickness and pain and death. We also need a better understanding of genuine faith. The real meaning of suffering has never been explained in a way that is universally satisfactory. Job, the oldest book in the Bible, delves into this question but gives us no final answer. Job goes no further than to say that we should not call God to account on this, but simply accept whatever He plans for us in His infinite wisdom.

I have observed suffering in many lives. I

have personally experienced the most tragic hurt that can come to us here in this world — the death of one who is very dear to us. I have known the dismal and hopeless finality of facing the tragic death of my daughter and having to go back and live in a world that can never, never be the same again.

But I have found that faith can act as a beacon and a sustaining force even in the darkest hour. Faith can help us pick up the pieces, rebuild, and go on. Faith can help us live for eternal values. I have found that some of the building blocks I need for the future are the blocks of pain of my past.

What I wish to present in the following pages is a Christian doctor's viewpoint on proper attitudes toward pain, sickness, death, and adversity. I hope to help some who may be confused about God's plan for their lives because illness has led them to feel God has rejected them. I hope to help some folks avoid the intense emotional and spiritual trauma that I have often seen in the sick, and in the friends and relatives of the dying.

I would like to share some ideas that have been meaningful to many of my patients — ideas that sustained me when tragedy in my family threatened my own spiritual equilibrium.

I hope this brief book will help you live victoriously and triumphantly in your hour of suffering.

Jonathan G. Yoder, MD

1

Adversity, Disease, and Decay

*Let me know how fleeting my life is! Be-
hold, thou hast made my days a few hand-
breadths, and my lifetime is as nothing in thy
sight. Psalm 39:4b, 5a.*

*Of old thou didst lay the foundation of the
earth, and the heavens are the work of thy
hands. They will perish, but thou dost endure;
they will all wear out like a garment. Psalm
102:25, 26a.*

Scientists have long told us that our whole
solar system is slowly getting colder and will
eventually die as other solar systems have.
Slowly, slowly mountains of the earth are
eroding away. The earth's energy resources are
steadily being used up. Humans thrive and be-

come physically stronger until their late twenties. Then their bodies join in the declining process. This is the ultimate tendency of the whole of the visible creation as we know it.

Adversity has been with us since the time of Adam. Genesis 1:28 tells us that God asked Adam to *subdue* and have dominion over everything on the earth. This command was given to Adam before Adam's sin and can only imply that there were hostile elements in the world when it was originally created by God. Adam was told to *subdue*. Subdue can have meaning only in the presence of hostility and opposition and adversity. These will always be with us.

Romans 8 indicates that *the whole physical creation was subjected to futility and decay because God willed it to be so.* The same chapter also tells us that God willed it to be so in order that the true eternal order may be revealed. From this decay of the physical God has promised to raise up something far more glorious.

Many ardent Christians are willing to accept some pattern of general adversity as part of God's will but they still are quite sure that the matter of good health is an exception. These folks would agree that we should not expect God to give us all our desires — that this would not be good for us. They would say that we should not expect God to give us all the money, all the sunshine, or all the fancy food and drink we might desire.

But some of these same Christians would

still say that God's children do have a right to total freedom from all disease. This is not consistent with the general pattern of adversity and decay that is built by God into the whole physical creation. Nor is this view of illness consistent with the lives of God's saints in the past, including Paul, who suffered a persistent physical ailment in spite of his prayers for healing.

Basically there is no real demarcation between human decay (getting old) and other human illnesses. "Infirmities" in old age, or "infirmities" in the more acute diseases of youth, all imply inability of our physical resources to cope with our bodies, tasks of promoting the well-being of our bodies in the face of opposition. So the infirmities of old age differ only in degree from the infirmities (or diseases) of the young.

As we become older our bodies lose their first ability to fight — the opposition to our good health becomes relatively stronger — and all of us eventually lose the battle. No person in perfect health ever dies. The process of "dying" begins before the age of 30. Aging and illness are a part of each other and both are a part of the path to decay which is shared by all of the visible creation — even by God's people.

We all know there are many verses in the Bible, especially in the Old Testament, that emphasize God's healing power. Often people quote Psalm 103:3 — "who heals all your diseases" — as proof that the righteous never need to be sick. But the same psalm mentions many physical blessings that God gives us. It does not focus on good health above the other blessings that God has for His children. The Old Testament does equate well-being, and prosperity in general, with a righteous life. But in no part of the Bible is good health set apart as a special sign of God accepting us as His children.

There are just as many Scripture verses about divine feeding as there are about divine healing. Still we concede that miraculous divine feeding is not a basic right of Christians, and that God's providing our daily bread is usually dependent on us working with our own hands for our food. In the New Testament we do not find any indication that a generally comfortable life is a sign of God's approval on our way of living. It seems that the New Testament actually stresses the opposite view. Over and over distress and suffering are listed as evidences of God's approval for our life.

Consider the Beatitudes in Matthew 5: "Blessed are the poor in spirit." "Blessed are those who mourn." "Blessed are those who are persecuted." Hebrews 12:6 has this same emphasis: "For the Lord disciplines him whom he loves, and chastises every son whom he receives." In 2 Corinthians 4:8-10 Paul said, "We are afflicted in every way, but not crushed; perplexed, but not driven to despair; persecuted, but not forsaken; struck down, but not destroyed. . . . So that the life of Jesus may also be manifested in our bodies."

14

Paul spoke of his own physical illness in 2 Corinthians 12, calling it his thorn in the flesh. God told him, "My power is made perfect in weakness." Then Paul responded, "I will all the more gladly boast of my weaknesses, that the power of Christ may rest upon me. For the sake of Christ, then, I am content with weaknesses, insults, hardships, persecutions, and calamities; for when I am weak, then I am strong."

Over and over again all of us have seen Christians make their most remarkable spiritual growth during periods of stress and suffering and not in times of prosperity and good health. I well recall the Thanksgiving services when my wife and I were serving in India. It was the custom of the Indian church to open the meeting for testimonies of blessings received during the past year. Most of these people were poor and all knew the meaning of the troubles of this world. But in this meeting the most meaningful testimonies always came from those who had suffered severe tragedy or illness in the past year.

I also recall a man I knew in college. I'll call him Jim. He was the happy-go-lucky type, apparently not interested in spiritual values. I lost track of Jim for many years. When I finally met him again, he had an excellent Christian family and was so much more mellowed and mature and interested in spiritual things than when I knew him in college days.

He told me about his son who had died

a few months before. The son had been born with a congenital heart defect, and for 14 years his family had been troubled and limited because of the physical weakness of this son who could never leave home. Countless nights had been spent hovering over him in illnesses. The whole family was never able to leave home together. Important meetings were missed, picnics were incomplete, and business was neglected because this son needed extra attention.

As he told me in a calm and deeply moving way about his son, I sensed that much of the spiritual growth and mellowing had come to Jim because of the 14 years of suffering.

I am aware that suffering sometimes produces bitterness in the one who suffers. But I believe such bitterness is produced by Christians who are only half committed. They are committed to God for only as long as God gives them the things that please them. They lack the faith to see that God can use the unpleasant things in life to bring them even greater blessings.

If you cannot accept suffering that comes from God without resentment, you are not a fully committed child of God. Even Christ was made "perfect through suffering" (Hebrews 2:10). So we are encouraged to expect suffering, but in it all to be triumphant. If Jesus needed suffering for His perfection, how much more we need it!

To all of this, I am compelled to add a personal testimony. God has been closest to me when I have experienced sorrow. The deep tragedies of my own life have been used by God to help me understand Him better. When I was weakest, I felt His strength most. God was closest to me when I found all my earthly resources utterly inadequate.

I believe that adversity and physical decay is inherent in the creation because God made it that way. As we have noted, Romans 8 and Genesis 1:28 indicate this is true. The disease germs I see under the microscope also confirm this idea. (The devil cannot create — not even germs.)

I find it confusing to agree that I need suffering for my spiritual growth, but that God is too kind to cause me to suffer and so He permits the devil to do it. What if I needed a serious surgical operation but my surgeon friend was too compassionate to do it for me! What if he had my worst enemy do the operation! In the Bible God does not refuse to take responsibility for the sickness and suffering we have, except for suffering that is the direct result of our own sins. Even Job accuses God repeatedly of causing his misery and God accepts full responsibility.

Suffering and decay of the physical, to reveal the eternal, are part of God's plan. Some people maintain that this is part of God's plan but that the devil carries it out within God's permitted limits. I'm not sure how God and the devil could "cooperate" in this way. Regardless, I am convinced that God is in full control of it all and, as in the Book of Job, accepts responsibility. If God accepts responsibility, it really doesn't matter much what agent carries out the course of events.

In some instances pain and sicknesses can be shown to be a direct result of our own sinful deeds or deliberately careless actions. This kind of suffering is not part of the will of God.

Death is our archenemy. From a human standpoint death represents the final victory of futility. Sickness and suffering are steps that lead to death. Human beings find it hard to accept the final physical victory of death. Many people tend to accept general adversity as a normal part of life, but refuse to come to terms with physical sickness.

Physical sickness and inevitable death go together! Christians should grasp the fact that these are God's agents for perfecting the soul and to "obtain the glorious liberty of the children of God" (Romans 8:21). In the life to come we will no longer find it hard to reconcile ourselves to God's plan for the physical creation. We will then see bodily weakness and decay as steps that lead to something much more glorious. This is our comfort.

"We know that the whole creation has been groaning in travail together until now; and not only the creation, but we ourselves, who have the first fruits of the Spirit, groan inwardly as we wait for adoption as sons, the redemption of our bodies" (Romans 8:22, 23).

"Though our outer nature is wasting away, our inner nature is being renewed every day. For this slight momentary affliction is preparing us for an eternal weight of glory beyond all comparison because we look not to the things that are seen but to the things that are unseen; for the things that are seen are transient, but the things that are unseen are eternal.

"For we know that if the earthly tent we live in is destroyed, we have a building from God, a house not made with hands, eternal in the heavens" (2 Corinthians 4:16 — 5:1).

When we fully accept the meaning of the above Scriptures the worst illnesses and even death will be seen in a different perspective.

2

The Quest for Healing

Bless the Lord, O my soul; and all that is within me, bless his holy name! . . . Who forgives all your iniquity, who heals all your diseases. Psalm 103:1, 3.

If sickness and suffering and decay are inherent in the creation, what can poor mortals do? It would appear that God's command in Genesis 1:28 to subdue the earth would apply to overcoming sickness along with mastering other aspects of our environment. God means for us to cross the rivers and the oceans, to conquer the lightning, and to subdue death-dealing germs.

I remember how thrilled I was in college when I first heard one of my professors relate the "parable" about God, Gabriel, and Benjamin Franklin. Benjamin Franklin was playing with a kite in a thunderstorm. Sparks flew from the string of the kite as Benjamin was experimenting. God watched like a fond parent. Suddenly God nudged Gabriel and said, "Look! Look! Benny's got it! Benny's got it!"

I've had a slight handicap all my life from the polio I experienced as a four-year-old. I've seen many tragic results from polio, both in children and adults. My own brother-in-law died of polio. Some years ago I had the special privilege of helping administer some of the research injections of Salk vaccine for polio. I well remember the thrill, mingled with awe, that caught me as I gave the first shot of vaccine. Could this be another breakthrough like Benjamin Franklin's? I wondered. Such breakthroughs are nurtured by God. Now that this vaccine has been found effective I continue to feel a bit of exuberance that I had even a very small part in conquering polio.

This same type of medical breakthrough has happened many times. Consider the discovery of the malaria germ, and subsequently the disease's remedy, quinine. Consider X-rays, new surgery techniques, antibiotics, vaccines, and many other medical advances. Only fifty years ago diphtheria was considered a scourge from God, and an epidemic of this disease caused panic in any community. Now diptheria does not exist except where people decline to accept the prevention that God has provided.

Some people will stumble at the assumption that diphtheria vaccine produces "God-provided" immunity. Such people insist that there is a sharp line of distinction between God-provided (or nature) cures and man-invented cures. We will discuss this in detail in the next chapter.

Still others would say that God-provided cures are only faith and prayer and never include medicine of any kind. They refer to many Scriptures which they feel support a rigid attitude of making no personal effort, except prayer, for healing. In their search for Bible verses that support this type of attitude such folks usually fail to note how the Bible treats sickness as a parallel to all other adversities of the physical world.

The Bible does teach that God gives us the healing we need, just as He gives us food and clothing and shelter. But for most of our physical needs we assume that God's promises to provide also imply that we will work with our hands and our heads to meet our physical needs. I find nothing in the Bible that indicates physical healing is a special need of ours, and that God expects us to expend no physical or mental effort for our physical healing.

The Bible says, "If any one will not work, let him not eat." This same rule applies to physical healing: "If any one will not work, let him not be healed." I have seen this demonstrated even in the lives of Christians who were ardent in their "faith" and claimed God's promises for healing, but who refused to use their own hands and heads to produce healing.

Some Christians draw a sharp line of demarcation, with doctors on one side and God on

22

the other. They feel that Christians cannot depend on both without seriously compromising their faith.

Christian doctors know better. We believe in divine healing because there is no other kind. We know that we ourselves have never ever healed anyone. We know how utterly dependent we are on God Himself for blessing our efforts and bringing something good from the little that we do. We know about the many, many times that He has guided and sustained us in our own weakness and even in our own confusion. So we humbly thank Him that He has seen fit to walk with us and often provides healing even when we have lost hope. We only plow the fields and plant the seeds, but God gives the increase.

And while we are talking about farmers we should also remember that we accept food from the hands of non-Christian farmers. These farmers think they themselves are the producers — not God. Still we accept their food. In the same way God may prepare medicine and care for us through doctors who do not acknowledge Him. We should accept such help as something that God has provided and thank Him for it all.

Some years ago a Christian drug salesman visited me at our India hospital. In the course of our conversation he told me his real attitude on medicine. Medicine, he said, was only for the weak in faith, not for those who were able to draw on God's power. He admitted that he was selling drugs for "weak" Christians and for the non-Christians, but he would never use medicine himself. Then he told me how God had worked in his life a few years previously.

He had experienced severe fever with chills and sweating. He stayed in bed and suffered and agonized with God. He prayed and he prayed but his faith held and he took no drugs. His pastor and friends came and prayed with him. He remained seriously ill for three months and was thought to be at the point of death one night. That night, suddenly something happened and he was abruptly healed. He had a striking testimony and he was fully convinced.

I told him that his symptoms seemed to indicate he had had malaria. I further suggested that God had provided the cure (atebrine) which was known to the patient. Likely God really wanted him to use the atebrine. If he had only taken it, he would have been well in three days instead of three months. But God finally relented. "All right, if you will not do it My way, I will do it yours." And then He healed the sick man.

God may at times honor our expressions of "faith" (or are they demands) because we see through a glass darkly. But this way of refusing God-provided help is not what the Lord intends. There is only one kind of healing — it is all divine healing, whether it arrives by the hands of a doctor or nurse or from the hands of a loving mother's care. Let us accept God's provisions for healing and be thankful.

3

Natural Medicine

*And God said . . . "Be fruitful and multiply,
and fill the earth and subdue it. Genesis 1:28.*

Before anyone knew about vaccination for
smallpox it was known that people who contracted cowpox became immune to smallpox.
This is a good example of one kind of natural
(or God-produced) immunity. Then it was found
that the smallpox virus does actually grow on
the cow but that the animal is less susceptible
to smallpox than man. So the cow gets only a
light form of the disease, which is called cowpox.

However, when the cow contracts cowpox it permanently damages and weakens the
smallpox virus so that it can never be strong
again. Then if people are exposed to this weakened virus they will only get cowpox. Their

body will learn how to fight cowpox and remain immune to cowpox. But the cowpox virus is enough like the smallpox virus that people who had the mild sickness of cowpox will also be immune to the severe sickness of smallpox. This was "nature's" way of making people immune to smallpox. This is "natural" vaccination.

But Jenner found that one could help "nature" along by purposely giving the smallpox virus to cows, and then removing the cowpox virus and giving the virus to people. So vaccination was discovered and we had one of those breakthroughs that have saved millions of lives. Still there are people who accept the milkmaid's natural immunity (after she had cowpox) as being from God, but who would object to vaccination because it is a man-made invention.

There is so much emphasis today about the "natural" being good and about the unnatural being of inferior quality. I agree that we have much to learn from the naturalists, but an overemphasis on the "natural" often produces serious misunderstanding about medicine. The damage from this type of misunderstanding is multiplied one hundredfold if only the "natural" is said to be God-given.

Can cowpox "vaccination" be all right if the milkmaid gets it without a doctor, by rubbing cows that have cowpox, but all wrong if someone "planted" it on the cow and then transferred the cowpox to the milkmaid to really vaccinate her? Is "natural" corn no longer good corn if I plant it in my garden and grow it under special conditions instead of allowing it to grow wild?

What is natural and what is not natural can be very closely related and really impossible to separate. God told Adam to subdue natural forces of the earth. This means to use these natural forces for the benefit of mankind. So we no longer ask whether corn is natural or not because we grow it in our garden. God expects us to use nature as our servant and not our master. Many medical breakthroughs have been based on this principle.

Years ago I took care of a poor man who got a small scratch on his hand while shoveling snow. It was only a superficial scratch at first, but the infection spread and spread. His arm swelled to three times its normal size. He suffered violent fever and chills, and after a few days died. He lived next door to my office, but I could do so little to help him. He died from a scratch.

I also remember the folks who had septicemia when I worked in the hospital as an intern. How we poor doctors floundered and worried in those days! I remember giving intravenous Mercurochrome, and what not, to kill the germs in the blood. But the patients died while we were frustrated and kept on floundering. Now we have penicillin. Just a wee bit of penicillin would have saved the life of that man with the scratch on his hand.

What is penicillin? Is it "natural" or manmade? Penicillin is a substance that fungi produce to protect themselves from bacteria. So it must be "natural." But we have discovered how to use this substance to protect ourselves from lethal bacteria. Dr. Flemming taught us how to grow the fungi and remove the penicillin and use it for ourselves. Is penicillin no longer a "natural" cure because we produce it in vats and put it in syringes for injection? Who knows if it is natural or unnatural? And what difference does it make if we accept God's command to subdue nature and use it for the benefit of mankind?

Smallpox vaccination is basically a means of subduing nature to secure immunity, like the milkmaid receives when she gets cowpox naturally. But by controlling this natural process we are able to give the benefits to millions by vaccination. I know the benefits of such vaccination. I have seen with my own eyes hundreds of smallpox-blinded people in India who were not vaccinated. I have seen some of the millions of deaths that have come to unvaccinated people. I have also seen the benefits to those who were vaccinated.

In much the same manner that is used to produce smallpox immunity, doctors have learned to give us immunity to other diseases. Many vaccines use live germs which have been weakened (like the cowpox virus) to induce our body to become immune to the real germ which is stronger than the weakened germ. Other vaccines use dead germs, or products of dead germs, to induce our body to be immune to the real germ.

28

All our bodies produce immunity by "natural" means. In the case of polio, people now have three choices of stimulus to cause their body to produce this natural immunity. If they choose not to be vaccinated the stimulus will likely be the strong natural polio virus that may leave them forever crippled, or may even kill them before their immunity becomes formed. Or they can choose Salk Vaccine, by injection, which consists of the dead polio virus. Even though it is dead it still stimulates the body to be immune thereafter to the strong and live virus. Or people may choose the oral vaccine which contains the weakened and ineffective live polio virus. We should not make an issue about which one is really natural. Indeed, if we refuse to "interfere with nature," we refuse to follow God's command to subdue the earth, which includes nature.

I have said much about vaccines as a method of using nature to promote our own well-being. I have tried to show that it may be difficult to find any basic difference between the immunity received "naturally" by milkmaids and immunity received from vaccination. Most of all, I have tried to show that it makes no difference, because God commanded us to use the earth and nature for our own well-being.

These same principles hold in other fields of medicine. Many herbs are used for medicine. Foxglove (the source of digitalis), quinine, cascara, and wintergreen are some of these. Many years ago foxglove tea was commonly thought to help people with heart trouble. Medical researchers found that the tea contained digitalis. Now drug houses extract the digitalis which is used instead of foxglove tea.

When we use digitalis we can take exactly the amount needed, because we know how much we are taking. But when we take foxglove tea we may die because we use too much or too little. Who will say foxglove tea is good because it is natural, and therefore from God, but a digitalis injection is of man and not of God?

Still further advancement of this type has enabled man (God guided them) to put together in the laboratory some of the exact substances that God provides in nature. Oil of wintergreen is one of the first natural products produced "artificially." Now some forms of penicillin are being put together in the laboratory. These synthetic drugs are often better than the natural drug for the particular task we wish to do. It is a part of God's plan that we imitate nature or even improve on it. Otherwise, who would plant a garden?

It is wonderful to subdue the earth and to be able to use the natural forces for the good of mankind. Harnessing electricity, propelling airplanes through the air, utilizing waterpower, extracting digitalis from foxglove to help heart patients, using deadly germs to defeat themselves when we make vaccines — all of these are part of God's plan for us.

I expect further breakthroughs under the guidance of God's hands — perhaps the cures for cancer and leukemia.

4

Miracles

*Shadrach, Meshach, and Abednego answered
the king, "O Nebuchadnezzar, we have no
need to answer you in this matter. If it be
so, our God whom we serve is able to deliver
us from the burning fiery furnace. . . . But
if not. . . ." Daniel 3:16, 17.*

I believe in miracles. But just a few days ago
a Christian woman remarked to me about people who claim miracles have happened in their
lives or in the lives of their friends. She
wondered why such cases always seem to
concern healing of illnesses of the body
or mind that cannot be proved or disproved
by anyone, even by doctors.

This lady is an ardent follower of Jesus. Just
a few moments before she had spoken of

God's guidance in her own life. She is not a skeptic — just a puzzled Christian. Might it be true that God follows patterns in His work — even in miracles? Also might it be that this Christian woman accurately stated the pattern regarding miracles today?

Consider the statement that miracles people report today are usually in areas that cannot be proved or unproved by anyone. Is this true? At first I decided not to write this book until I had done considerable research on this point. I composed letters to the most prominent faith healers in America requesting extensive details and supporting data about my cases of provable miracles of healing. Then I packed the letters away and never sent them. I decided that this is not something that it is appropriate to prove or disprove at all.

The point still is true, however, that I have never seen a leukemia case cured, nor an empty eye socket receive a new seeing eye, nor an arm or leg growing back to replace an amputated limb, and so on. In fact, I have never seen any healing miracle that could be measured and proved in any way. Not only this, but I have never even talked with anyone who claims to have seen such a miracle and wished for it to be analyzed, proven, and documented. Many confused Christians have ardently wrestled with the Lord for a miracle that was outside His usual pattern. The most sincere and honest Christians have come to soul-shaking crisis over this kind of "faith" (or shall we say hope?).

Few who read this (perhaps none) will be able to say that they know of a definitely proved, measured, and documented miracle. Why do Christians then search so frantically for the kind of miracles that God does not usually see fit to perform in these modern days. Is it because all present-day Christians are weak and wavering? I do not think so.

The Bible says that the physical creation, as we know it, is in the process of decay and destruction. Romans 8:18-23 teaches that God planned it this way so that eternal values may come out of this perishing physical creation. Perhaps the degenerating state of our physical bodies is a direct result of man's original choice not to follow God fully.

Regardless of the original cause of our tendency to decay, this cause is no longer reversible. None of us are able to reverse the physical consequences of the Fall of Adam for ourselves or for anyone else by living free from sin. So we will not pursue further the question of the "why" of sickness. We will examine what attitude we should take toward disease and decay which according to God's plan will eventually produce eternal good and a glorious victory.

In spite of the promise of eternal life for Christians after death, all of us find ourselves very much like the minister I once heard say, "I don't want to die, and I am not going to die as long as I can keep from it." He seemed to be in perfect health at the time, but died five months later.

33

I too enjoy living! Friends, flowers, breezes, birds, mountains, travel, tasks to accomplish — all these make life enjoyable. So we don't want to die. We refuse to die as long as we can avoid it.

Because all of us are enthralled by the good things God has given us in this life, sometimes we ask God to modify His usual pattern of working and make an exception for us. So we ask for a miracle.

All diseases can be placed in two classes: (1) organic diseases and (2) functional diseases. Organic diseases are those in which the mind or will of the patients has no part, either in the origin of the disease, or in its course thereafter. Functional diseases are caused by the mind or emotions of the patient. In the strictest sense, these diseases have no organic or anatomical basis. It is not always clear which diseases fall into which category. Many diseases that are strictly organic at the onset may change to functional diseases because of improper treatment and wrong attitudes.

The causes of organic diseases can usually be demonstrated by laboratory findings, X-rays, or distinctive signs which we can document. Basic functional diseases cannot be demonstrated, although often organic changes that follow can be demonstrated. It does appear that miracles of healing frequently occur in the realm of functional diseases, but very, very rarely in the realm of organic diseases. Since functional diseases cannot be demonstrated, miraculous healing of these diseases cannot be demonstrated and documented. Further, since miraculous healing of organic disease very, very rarely occurs, documentation of such cases is not likely. If we wish to prove and measure and document miracles of healing, we will be disappointed.

Let us consider briefly why God may not choose to heal miraculously organic diseases that come to us from forces entirely outside our control. Some of us would say that such organic diseases must be considered part of the general pattern of decay that has been in effect since creation. Some would say it is there because of sin. I do not know, but Hebrews 2:10 says that even sinless Jesus was made perfect through suffering. So regardless of the original cause of suffering, we mortals can not expect to escape suffering even if we live a perfect life like Jesus did. We need some suffering for our own good.

Adversity and pain are part of God's present plan for all of His loved ones. "If you are left without discipline, in which all have participated, then you are illegitimate children and not sons" (Hebrews 12:8). So when we ask God to cure us miraculously of organic disease we are asking Him to contradict Himself. We are asking Him to modify His basic plan for the universe. Usually God does not choose to do so.

Even Jesus prayed earnestly for God to change His basic plan: "Father, if thou art willing, remove this cup from me· nevertheless not my will, but thine, be done" (Luke 22:42). But God was not willing and Jesus accepted God's plan.

Functional diseases, however, are not a part of the basic pattern of built-in adversity and decay. They are due to faulty attitudes, emotional stresses, and sometimes to sin. God wants to help us get rid of these things. So miracles of healing do occur frequently for functional diseases.

Some readers will take exception to the statement that miracles of healing that can be measured, proved, and documented are very, very rare. Religious periodicals frequently report miraculous healing of organic diseases. A church periodical I read reported such a miraculous healing some years ago. No further information about the "healed" individual was printed until 18 months later when her obituary appeared in the same paper. It reported that she was ill and bedfast for the last year and half of her life.

Another "miracle" mentioned in this same paper was a case of permanently cured leukemia. When asked for details, the writer became annoyed and refused to furnish any follow-up information.

Just yesterday I read a Christian optometrist's reaction to a reported healing of vision: "They just don't want to wear glasses anymore so they consider themselves 'healed.' I have checked them many times, and they still have the same 20/70 vision as they had before. You might just as well talk about growing a new arm from the shoulder or growing a new eye in an empty socket, as changing lost vision in this sudden and miraculous way."

The Catholic Church has long been known for its many shrines of healing. Hundreds of thousands of people visit these shrines every year. In order not to mislead people who are sick, the Catholic Church has set up study groups to document and prove any cases that are said to be outstanding and evident miracle healings. These groups find very, very few cases that really can be documented as authentic. Protestant faith healers, I fear, would not have a better record if a scientific study were done.

People often become possessed with a frantic desire for healing from a disease to which they cannot reconcile themselves. Miracles are often "claimed" and reported, but an unbiased study would say they are still sick. Periodicals that print these reports are seldom informed of later developments. Retractions of claimed miracles are not announced nor printed.

Afflicted people should avoid self-condemnation because they are ill, and false hope of receiving healing as one of God's promises. Real faith goes far beyond having all our desires granted.

We should be very careful when we ask God to set aside His general pattern and basic plan because we are an extra-special case. I have heard the slogan, "Expect a miracle." If this means that we should expect God to change His regular pattern of working, because we know better, then it is a bad slogan. At any rate, events that are expected, are no longer considered miraculous — however wonderful they are — like the birth of a baby! Expected miracles would lose their awe.

What can we do to meet the need of the Christian who is stricken with what would appear to be an uncurable organic disease? I would suggest that the first message should be, "Be still and see if God has a message for you." At a time like this it is difficult to hear God. Instead of listening for what God has to say, we tend to respond, "It can't happen to us" and frantically try to prove that God does not really intend this condition for us. Then we try to induce God to work the miracle that has been agreed on as "God's will." We talk and talk to God so desperately we may never hear what God is trying to say to us.

I have seen numerous tragic and traumatic endings to this kind of approach. Since miracles that can be verified and documented are exceedingly rare, is there any special reason that I should receive a different response from God than the other millions of His children?

We mortals are finite. In the light of eternity, we cannot comprehend what experiences will help us most. When we are sick and weak we may be especially disturbed and unable to discern the will of God for us. But even when we are well our knowledge is so limited.

I have performed many operations on children less than two years old. I caused them pain. They could not understand why. Most of all they could not understand why their parents, whom they thought loved them deeply, had let the doctor hurt them. I submit that compared to our heavenly Father our understanding is less than that of a two-year-old. We will never fully understand. But we know our Father and that is enough.

5

Healing of the Mind

Create in me a clean heart, O God, and put a new and right spirit within me. Psalm 51:10.

It has long been known that the mind often has a profound effect on the body during the course of disease. Many years ago it was noted that young people who experienced severe disappointments in love more frequently contracted fatal tuberculosis than others. Emotional factors are closely related to some diseases such as stomach ulcers, asthma, types of arthritis, warts, chronic skin ailments, some baldness, allergies of all kinds, and many other physical disorders. Cures of some organic diseases may be secondary to securing the good mental and emotional attitudes of the individual.

A warning, however, is in order. We must not assume that *all* sickness is because of the mind. An amputated limb, a decayed tooth, all diseases of heredity, and most germ diseases are not diseases that can be radically influenced by emotional factors. No one fully knows where to draw the line between functional and organic factors, but we know that emotions have a tremendous influence on the course of many diseases. Therefore, healing of the mind and the emotions is a most powerful influence in healing many (but not all) bodily diseases. It is my conviction that it is in this area where the actual miracles of healing occur.

Now I know that immediately many people will say, "But these are not miracles. The people aren't really sick. It's only in their minds. There is really nothing wrong."

I seriously challenge the statement that people with psychosomatic illness really have nothing wrong with them. Nothing wrong? But their soul is in turmoil and their mind has no peace! Nothing wrong? But their innermost consciousness does not have the foundation of a meaningful life or any assurance of a purpose or calling. Nothing wrong? But they have nothing to live for, and if necessary, to die for.

When basic ideas are wrong, everything is wrong. So hate, anxiety, insecurity, and envy take over and a stomach ulcer develops. Then such a victim of hate has an encounter with God and his basic attitudes change miraculously. The stomach ulcer heals in a

41

short time. I maintain this is a miracle — a miracle of mind healing — and body healing follows.

Skeptics may further insist, "But it is only in your mind." What do you mean when you say it is *only* in your *mind*? People who say this fail utterly to comprehend what it is to be really sick. The Bible emphasizes that the one sickness that matters most of all is sickness of the spirit. Diseases of the mind and soul directly affect the physical body now, but they also affect one's eternal well-being.

Notice how often Jesus healed the minds and hearts of the ill before He restored their physical health. One such example is recorded in Matthew 9:1-8. Here Jesus healed a paralytic of sins and sickness of his mind. Then, when many doubted that He had power to forgive sins, He performed the visible miracle to prove His power to perform the invisible miracle. Jesus' own words indicate that He attached greater importance to the inward miracle than to the outward healing.

Christians have always believed that heart-and-soul healing can be instantaneous. This is the essence of the Christian message of hope — even for the dying. When this kind of healing takes place suddenly and miraculously, often some related diseases will soon also disappear. Whether such diseases are labeled psychosomatic or not makes no real difference in the end. These are miracles that the scientific world cannot see and document. But Christians see them and know about them.

It would seem then that there are two types of suffering. Organic disease and suffering are a part of the creation that God has given man to "subdue." The other kind of suffering is that of the soul and mind. God will often heal this kind of disease instantly for people who truly wish Him to do so. Christians should expect the hidden miracles resulting from a healing of the spirit. They should not be perturbed that miracles that can be documented and proven do not occur in these days.

God promised us peace of mind and forgiveness. We are glad for any physical healing that may follow. But God never promised Christians an easier physical life because they are Christians. And if we have the peace that Christ gives to us, physical miracles do not matter that much after all. To illustrate this statement, let me share the story of one of my patients.

Mary (not her real name) was only thirty years old at the time. Her husband was engaged in full-time church service. They were the parents of five young children. She came to my office because she had a lump in her breast. It was obvious to me that the lump should be examined further, so I sent her to the hospital for a biopsy and possible removal of the breast. At the time of surgery preliminary tests showed that the lump probably was cancerous. Not only was Mary's breast involved, but also nearby glands. So radical surgery was performed on this young wife and mother.

A lot of conflicts swirl through a doctor's

mind at a time like this. After the operation I told Mary what it looked like and also what the tests showed at the time of surgery. But I also stalled a bit for time. I told her we would not be absolutely certain she had cancer until the final studies after surgery were done, and that these reports would not be back for several days.

Three days later the reports were waiting for me at the hospital and indicated a very malignant form of cancer. I took considerable time at Mary's bedside so we could talk things over together. We discussed the way many Christians react to such a crisis, crying frantically for a miracle.

Then I reminded Mary of the three Hebrew children who were about to be thrown into the blazing furnace. They had the faith to say that whether or not a miracle was forthcoming was not really important. They trusted God and knew He was in control, and that was enough.

I stopped to see Mary again the next day. She was calm and unruffled. I apologized for breaking the bad news to her when she was alone the day before. But she thanked me for having told her. "I couldn't sleep for three nights because of uncertainty and worry," she said. "Last night I slept perfectly."

Truly, if we have the peace that only Christ can give, physical miracles don't matter that much, after all. But Mary's story would not be complete if I did not add a "progress note" after 17 years. Mary and her family have moved to a distant city. In the past few years there have been recurrences of her cancer. But Mary is thankful. God spared her to raise her children to adulthood. Was there a miracle? Who knows! After all, God cares for His own and all of life is a miracle.

6

The Perspective of Faith

By faith Abraham obeyed . . . and he went out, not knowing where he was to go. Hebrews 11:8.

To me, Hebrews 11 and 12 are the chapters in the Bible that I find most thrilling and awe-inspiring. These chapters give us the faith to live in triumph, regardless of events that some would call calamities. If we read carefully we will note that many of these heroes of faith never received in their own lifetimes the things they are said to have "received" by faith.

How different this is from some of our modern-day teaching that faith means getting what we asked for! Skeptics would say that the saints of Hebrews 11 settled for "pie in the sky by and by." But these heroes would have responded differently. Hebrews 11 says unseen things had been seen, had been received, and had been embraced. What a paradox — having without having!

"Now faith is the substance of things hoped for" (Hebrews 11:1, KJV). Substance is something I can handle and feel. Faith allows me to hold things I cannot touch.

"What is seen was made out of things which do not appear" (Hebrews 11:3). Here again we have "substance" that has been made from nothing.

"These all died in faith, not having received the promises, but . . . were persuaded of them, and embraced them" (Hebrews 11:13, KJV).

How can you embrace something you do not have? How could Abraham have his security, his city with *foundations* while he was living in fragile tents that were forever being uprooted and torn by the wind? How could Abraham embrace his land of inheritance when he was living in the desert sands? How could he embrace his multitude of descendants when he had no child at all? But this passage says that Abraham embraced his descendants and his inheritance and his city with foundations when he didn't have any of them.

Moses "considered abuse suffered for the Christ greater wealth than the treasures of Egypt. . . . He endured as seeing him who is invisible" (Hebrews 11:26, 27). More pie in the sky! Moses saw something that simply wasn't there!

Seeing the invisible! Thomas just couldn't do it. He had to see with his physical eyes. Jesus did bless him but called his attention to a higher and better kind of faith. It's nice to have faith so we can handle rattlesnakes or to perform other miracles we can see with our eyes. But Jesus told Thomas of a higher faith that does not require these visible manifestations.

Moses had this better faith. He saw something that gripped and motivated him to triumphant living for all his life. So Moses denounced everything that the world counted valuable in order to claim what he saw by faith. He claimed it for his daily living, not just for the distant future — spiritual victory in the midst of reproach and sorrow.

Moses received what he wanted without actually obtaining it. What a paradox! He accepted it by faith. How different from what so many tell us who say faith means getting what you ask for! Even Jesus, in Gethsemane, did not get what He asked for.

What does the Bible really teach us about really triumphantly living in faith? Hebrews 11 tells us that faith does not usually enable us to foretell the future and predict a particular favorable outcome. It tells us that we need not worry about the future. How often Christians equate faith with the ability to foretell a favorable outcome for a present illness. Abraham "went out, not knowing where he was to go." He did not know the outcome; he only knew his Leader, and that was enough. Abraham proceeded to offer up Isaac, confident that God was able to raise him from the dead, but he just did not know what God had in mind.

This same element of faith — trusting God without knowing what He will do — is reflected many times in the Bible. The three Hebrew children in the Book of Daniel, who were about to be cast into the furnace, said they were sure God could deliver them. But they also admitted they were not sure God would deliver them. Their confidence that God was able to deliver them was all they needed to feel secure, unwavering, and victorious. Whatever was about to happen to them was of secondary importance. "Having faith" did not mean assurance of deliverance from the furnace.

We also have the examples of the many sick people who came to Christ for healing. *Christ did not ask them if they had faith that they were going to be healed.* He did ask many of them if they had faith that He was able to heal them. What a difference! This is the approach of humble supplication to Almighty God whose power we know and whose goodness we trust.

If we really trust Him we will no longer feel that it is only we who know the proper outcome for our present difficulty. Job said, "Though he slay me, yet will I trust in him" (Job 13:15, KJV). To trust Him completely, regardless of outcome, may require more genuine faith than to assert vehemently that we know we are going to be healed.

This may especially be true for patients (or the families of patients) who are known to have an illness that is usually considered incurable. People who are struck with such illnesses may find themselves unable to cope with this adversity and susceptible to teachings about faith that are not according to the Bible.

When medical people tell us we have an incurable disease God may be trying to talk to us. We should listen to Him. But instead we may start a one-way conversation with God and talk so forcefully and so long that He never has a chance to reveal Himself to us. This is not the faith we read of in Hebrews 11. Faith does not give us ability to foretell the outcome of our crisis.

Hebrews 11 and 12 tell us clearly that faith is not a sure way to secure what we judge to be a favorable outcome to our trouble. Please note the following contrasts in outcome for heroes of faith in Hebrews 11:34-37:

Some quenched the violence of fire and escaped the edge of the sword; some were stoned and sawn in two.

Some became mighty in war and put foreign armies to flight; some suffered chains and imprisonment.

Women received their dead raised to life again; some were destitute, afflicted, and ill-treated.

Clearly faith does not necessarily produce physical healing and physical deliverance. Hebrews 12:5-11 goes still further, telling us to expect chastening and discipline as evidence of God's love, and as an indication that He has accepted us as His children. If we have faith, the physical outcome is of relatively minor importance. Faith enables us to look beyond the immediate affliction to the invisible and the eternal. We will bow our hearts in awe and accept God's plan for us. "This is the victory that overcomes the world, our faith" (1 John 5:4).

7

Is That All?

If a man die, shall he live again? Job 14:14.
Then I saw a new heaven and a new earth.
Revelation 21:1.

Her name was Mary Jean — our daughter —
fragile, dedicated, sincere, and vulnerable.
During her short life Mary Jean proceeded on
the conviction that she was here for a purpose
and for a plan. She tried hard to find God's
special plan for her life. For a time she tried
to find it by disciplining her body. She slept on
the hard floor and went without food. She
rose early in the morning and spent an
hour or two searching for God's will before
she began her studying.

Later, when Mary Jean felt God told her to
study medicine she called off her previous work

and went all out studying medicine. Even while she struggled through medical school she found time for two hours of early morning prayer and meditation. One of her medical schoolmates said of her, "She was one of God's saints, walking this earth." But her life was marked by many agonizing struggles, and weeping, in search of God's will for her life.

Eventually Mary Jean graduated with high honors and received her medical degree. Five days later she departed this life. We buried her in a plot, two feet by six feet. Physically, she is gone from this life forever. Is that all? Is that all for a lifetime of struggle, self-discipline, and hard work?

All of us have experienced the letdowns that often follow the realization of some long-sought goal. Deep inside of us we may wonder, "Is that all?"

Long ago a poet said:
But pleasures are like poppies spread;
You seize the flower, the bloom is shed.

Many of life's goals become like empty stems of poppy flowers when we finally have them in our hands. The petals drop off even as we seize them. So we sit and look at the empty stem and wistfully ask, "Is that all?"

Moses could have asked that too after his long life as he was dying. He had turned his back on a chance to become Pharaoh for the sake of a dream — a calling. He had experienced hardship in return — a life of criticism, blame, and often failure. Now at the end of his life the temperamental children of Israel are still in the wilderness. He is about to die. "Is that all?"

It was also thus for Abraham. He left everything and followed a vision — or was it an illusion? In the end he was still living in his flapping old tents in the sandstorms of the desert. He had spent all his life looking for a city with foundations. At his death in the same torn tents in which he had struggled all his life, Abraham could have asked, "Is that all there is?"

Today the physical is so real and evident to us. The unseen — well, we believe about eternal values but they are far away. Whenever our goals and our efforts are for only physical and visible ends, the answer always comes back, "Yes, that is all." The two-by-six burial plot is all that remains of our vast holdings — the final fruit of all our struggles and our pains and our weeping. But for those who have eternal goals, there is more. Their lives, their work, their witness go on. Like Moses and Abraham, they have built for eternity.

In this world there is pain, sickness, decay, and death. Is that all? Is that the final result of striving for ultimate values. No, we have been created with eternity in our hearts. Mankind has always cried, "Yea, the work of our hands establish thou it" (Psalm 90:17). God has promised that the work we do for Him in this world will bear everlasting fruit. He has promised us everlasting life — life that begins here and now and goes on forever and ever.

Change and decay are here, but thank God, this is not all. Eternal life is a gift from God and all of us can realize such a life.

The Author

Jonathan G. Yoder, MD, has devoted much of his life to medical work in India. He was born on a farm in Elkhart County, Indiana, and received his education at Middlebury High School, Goshen College (BS, 1927), and Indiana School of Medicine (MD, 1933).

Ordained as a Mennonite minister, Dr. Yoder and his wife and baby daughter, Joanne Yvonne, sailed for India as missionaries. They served there from 1937 to 1945 and again from 1947 to 1953.

"During our first term," Dr. Yoder recalls, "two new members joined our family. Mary Jean arrived in 1939. Richard arrived in 1942 and died seven hours after birth. I had the very traumatic experience of being the doctor as well as the father when Richard was born and died. In 1948 the Lord gave us our third daughter, Ruth Elaine.

"We returned to the United States in 1953 to preserve our family living while our oldest children finished high school and college. I split my time between providing for our children's education and maintaining our family ties in the United States, on the one hand, and our medical missionary call to the Orient, on the other hand. Mary Jean died in an auto accident, in 1964, five days after she received her own MD degree.

"Since 1953 I have completed four short assignments in India and Nepal that varied from one to three years. I am presently on another short-term assignment in Nepal. While in the United States I practice medicine in Goshen and Middlebury, Indiana.

"I have some sad memories and scars, but through it all I see the Lord at work. I have also had a basically happy and fulfilling life. Joys of fulfillment outweigh the disappointments we Christians have. I am happy for the life He has given me."